The Body in Space

ALSO BY GERRIE FELLOWS

Technologies and Other Poems (Polygon, 1990)
The Powerlines (Polygon, 2000)
The Duntroon Toponymy (Mariscat, 2001)
Window for a Small Blue Child (Carcanet, 2007)

Gerrie Fellows

The Body in Space

Shearsman Books

First published in the United Kingdom in 2014 by
Shearsman Books
50 Westons Hill Drive
Emersons Green
BRISTOL
BS16 7DF

Shearsman Books Ltd Registered Office
30–31 St. James Place, Mangotsfield, Bristol BS16 9JB
(this address not for correspondence)

www.shearsman.com

ISBN 978-1-84861-343-0

ACKNOWLEDGEMENTS

Thanks are due to the editors of the journals, online journals and
anthologies in which some of these poems first appeared: *New Writing
Scotland;* http://skying-blog.blogspot.co.uk/; *the Journal of Postcolonial
Writing; Stravaig; Island; Nomad; Cutting Teeth; West Coast Magazine; Back to
the Light. New Glasgow Poems,* edited by Donny O'Rourke and Hamish
Whyte, Mariscat Press/Glasgow City Council, 2001; *The Hand That Sees.
Poems for the Quincentenary of the Royal College of Surgeons of Edinburgh,*
edited by Stewart Conn, RCSEd/Scottish Poetry Library, 2005.

'Birds Enter It' was published by the Tramway alongside the exhibition,
Unreliable Witness, as part of a project with the first Clydebuilt Verse
Apprentices of whom I was the mentor in 2008-9. Thanks are due to
Simon Biggam of *Glasgow Life* and to Jim Carruth of *Mirrorball.*

'The Language of Memory (The Bees)' was a winner in the
2012 Troubadour International Poetry Competition.

My particular thanks to Elizabeth Burns, David Kinloch,
Tom Leonard and Gerry Loose.

Contents

I. The Miraculous World

II. At the Aliens' Gate

III. Petroglyphs

IV. Lucky Heart

V. The Language of Memory

I

The Miraculous World

The Miraculous World

From a bothy
spun around a pole   odd tree
in a place without wood
its sills, shells   its windows
onto water and the cliff
where our men lean outward
roped over waves

she watches her father climb
through the sheared air
holds him in her sight
out over the dark   all I saw of the minke
triangular fins of coasting sharks
the gannets' dive   the explosion
that comes to us across the water

At the end of his route
he'll show her a pinioned boulder
triangle of air   she might
step through: we'll hold her
in the net of our observation   unroped
in a place sheeny with quartz and salt
that slants away

            to the waves'
white rushing and falling back
the sharks' dark fins
the ballet of gannets
their light bones   their perfectly
aerodynamic skulls   diving into
all around us
the miraculous world

From Breanais

I

At Uig   building a mountain
a castle, a harbour
my daughter's bridge
the only one that will stand
in the wet sand

towers are brochs
fallen into ruin
even as they're built   a rubble
like the concrete blocks
left standing
the roofless houses

From the back of the beach
she yells urgently over and over
what is this?

pellet knit with fur and rabbit bones
the knuckles as clear
as if just lifted
from the broth of the stomach

What bird   coasting on great wings
gurgled this knot   disgorger
over the machair
over eyebright and sandwort
bird's-foot trefoil

II

What bird
coasting on great wings

over half-built dwellings
     hump-backed houses fallen back
to walls the hurricane filled up with sand

     stones   flung above a beach
   (the way a hurricane enters a conversation)

     places revealed by storm
     places sealed and hidden

over the dead buried at the edge of the ocean

III

The custodian is telling us
how fish and seal meat, seabirds
     smoked above a hearth
were stored in the cool stone cellar
how smoke drifts from the hearth
how she brushes the ashes out
        day after day
   in a house set down in earth
The English she speaks is smoky with Gaelic sounds
(as if it had in it a colour found only in this place)

   orchid   clover   tufted vetch
   heath milkwort   siabann nam ban-sìdh
   forget-me-not   cotharach   protector

   her purple cardigan   like a flower of the machair

IV

Mealisval, Cracaval,
Laival a' Tuath, Laival a' Deas, Griomaval

They might be the names
of colours
in a poem about light
shades of blue
when the sky
is a clear, subtle turquoise

shades of translucence
when the ocean
is a green mineral
light/ness of elements
suspended between wave lengths

V

Even on Leòdhas they say it—
Breanais is the back of beyond

a house with yellow like the eye
or the beak of a bird
as if a great seabird
ground-nested there
coasting   watching the ocean

In the grass of the machair
the head and beak of a fulmar
the beak intact   ochre
the closed curve of a knife
broken-open   empty skull
delicate   white
almost translucent

This is what we found

The bones of birds
are lighter than ours

Island Journal

I

Walking on Mull's basaltic sands
we look aslant   over water
    from our wet footprints
the way the lava ran
    from the caldera   molten

    to the slate islands' riven fins
Cullipool's black steep
that pitched our daughter's football once
    from beach

    to wave tips   white on white
    taking the yachts' sails
against the lava flow
    from that island
cattle-grazed with green

    to this island's cooled opposite
to our being here now
aslant in time and distance
bound   by black sand   by water

II

After rain: you and I
over moss   water-logged pasture
    steep up into the
rain diary   logged rainbows
sharp showers   sharp
wind   dipping below the cloud
of our big dark neighbour

but we're on fire
the caldera's flow fixed to stone
    cold, but we are warm-
blooded animals   moving
in the bellow of stags
scree travellers   footing it
    over and up   looking back

at the distant col   at unexpected
others   might be rocks
but their legs jolt as they stand
I expect them   silhouetted
crossing the ridge   but
    they are nowhere
our co-inhabitants   vanished
into the planet of time and rock

III

Gone over water
he travels towards his father
fallen flyer on Warfarin

She and I at a forest edge
talking of this
between upheaved tussocks
grass, pathless   bracken
the conversation of years:

beyond us, unseen   the debris
of a wartime flight   ripped
aluminium in rock   a vanishing
as of walkers on a ridge   or the flit
of yesterday's texts on her phone

    our bootprints trackless
    on the steep black scree

IV

At the boat rail
our daughters

mottled as young birds
as seal pups
        out on the water

towards a landing stage
        light-stepped
                pyramid

        out towards
                bird churches
broken lava terraces

        out towards

And where we were
        a green falling away

V

a walk by raised beaches   sheep
fort   verdant headland in rain
taking us by columns cooled
to the hexagonal   the not-quite
we marvel at   dark honeycomb
        over which the sea escapes

racing away from us
        as the beaches lift
                tip us   descending

      towards fanned basalt
flattered by sunlight

A child's delight
at the monkey puzzle shape of it
dashed to a stump   hollow impress
of a trunk   gigantic horsetail
    up beyond us,   craning necks
    until I say to her—
    fifty million years

    standing as we do
    in the Atlantic forests
    in the warm damp
    young as we are   in the ancient

The Invisible Field

Beyond a gate emblazoned with padlocks
in a ghost territory of bracken and fencing
bootsoles smash downwards on concrete
and powerlines burr under the arch of pylons

Where the shepherd had a house from the master
two cows' grass   pasture for sixty sheep on the hill
chainsaws fell upright stands of conifer
for chipboard   cellulose   rayon   newsprint
for boxes   fences   telegraph poles

The graziers were at first considered by the natives
as aliens and invaders of property
Abortive attempts were made to extirpate them

The soil of the plantings   rain-washed downwards
leached   ash grey   iron pan on the slopes
(salt and earth kept separate on the breast of the corpse)
the alkali of the spirit
the destructible granular body   graded and quarried

concrete   uplifted by mountains
where ice cup was   *argent*   spillage of cold
rasped over quartz mica
All this broken through   *a saltire   engrailed*
(The crest   a demi-savage
brandishing in his dexter hand a broadsword)

A torse of rock crushed and sectioned
one hundred and fifty tons an hour transported
across submerged and treacherous regions
mixed with sand became the healing balm
on cableways slung from headmasts
three thousand cubic yards a week

eight and a quarter miles of concrete aqueducts
a hundred and four intake dams
section by section   the headwall
thirteen buttresses spanned by arches
In an escroll above   the motto THIS I'LL DEFEND

Upright upon the earth   the engineer
calculated the meanings of rock and water
*Let concrete be the balm   Let water run
in the penstocks   Let energy equal light*

Supporters   two highland men in belted plaids
in trenches of rock and mud
incomers from war   at war with the earth
rainwashed   slipping beneath them
(the cast-off cladding the falling timber
the men bare-headed sweating shaken)
(anonymous but for the injured and the dead)

Section by section   the headwall
a memorial plaque one hundred and sixty feet high
*all Proper   standing on a compartment wavy
whereon is the word LOCH SLOY*

The slung cables sigh under the arch of pylons
The invisible field dwarfs the bungalow
a man and a woman fenced and netted
bodies disrupted   as mine is
passing beneath that charged singing

*Let there be light in the dark regions
an end to black Mondays on Clydeside
an end to blackouts on washday in the tenements*

And there was light: far down Glen Loin
it burns over the nuclear secrets
over the shipwrecked yards
over my own boots on the road

Trajectory

From the summit to a corner
of fence and forest   coordinates
an odd scatter   mineral pages
pitted grey-green among conifers
the eroded aluminium folios
of a B29   its buckled shiners
among knuckles of yellow quartz
on the peat-stained hillside

a place I want to call a grave site
though no one's buried here
the dead inscribed on a metal plaque
and a photograph
left in memory and loss
of a young man on an airfield
sixty years ago   casually astance
more faded than the tiny, furled flag
in the name of which
so much has been committed
his country's history   mine

this wintry hillside
the rough rock memorial
the unspoken names
not written on the beautiful debris
on the sheafed silvery turbines
    of each engine
    frozen here in folded waves

    on the flattened pipes
and the black rubber window seal
of the pressurised cabin
    that allowed it to fly
    way above fighter planes

(Over Hiroshima   Nagasaki
nothing could touch them
the first high altitude bombers)

What was it doing in deep Argyll?
After the Berlin airlift
(food not death in the big hold)
flying home into a winter forecast
(nothing could touch it)   zero
visibility   the risk of icing

inverted evidence of aftermath
metal   delicate instruments
bodies of young men going home
heaved over into fire and bog
wheel rim   rusted landing gear
a shock absorber   still shining
     among the sphagnum
and snow-smattered tussocks

where sixty years later we crouch
in our layers of fleece and Gore-tex
in this sun-wintered litter of metal
among scrabbled cables
     twisted to functionless parts

in scattered snow on a fierce bright day
over us   two rising jet trails

II

At the Aliens' Gate

In the Small Hours (Night Document)

I

We float in billowing umbra
Furniture cradles us
You dream in its wooden hands

Through the chill hallway
I find myself   in the small hours
at the kitchen table   above me
the pulley festooned with washing
the gas burning blue and rose

This is your home   these spaces
the years   footsteps
echoing over them

Into it   I entered
after so many lives
a woman in my thirties

Nothing is pure   Nothing in my life
may tell its form as plainly as
a spoon turned in a faceted glass
or the swirled cusp of a bowl

I walked through flames of bracken
broken stalks   beaten down by rain
before I met you

II

At the end of a decade of internments
the self turned in
to family   that bastion of echoes

generation after generation intoning
inheritance is love

Yet we have been cocooned
as fellow creatures   together
under the sharp chill stars
Loveliness   turning its limpid water
over the Etive stones   Sunlit
ourselves   the roped climbers
over granite   the many points
of brightness

Here all was open   all connection
perspective   possibility

III

South   my sister   home from work
in the early dark rummages for keys
on the metal skeleton of the steps
A country and a train ride between us
we've talked of the living struggle
embattled   patching together
the possible

My mother   in her London backyard
in the season of fog   has set ablaze
dry leaves and the stump of a dead tree
telling me this over the wires
northward   meaning   something is burnt
Something is finished in the old season

Are we still searching for the tell-tale
line of hills   brash   open   echoing
our own country?

Here November is a month of frost
of water frozen in the runnels   the red
tenements burning under cerulean blue
A month of clarity

IV

I chose to live in Scotland
for reasons of hope in a dark decade
yet it's a strange country to have chosen
the female   a mythic ship
made on Clydeside in the past of men

Or did the country choose   saying
here is the cleat of your boot
embedded in the black peat

taught me to listen to its language?

And I have learned to listen
to hear it   shriller   each year
grown harsher

What country is this
and what could I say of it?
I am a stranger
speaking another language

V

And yet here in the small hours
I place myself   in history

Lifting the blind onto the deep well
of November night   over it the stars

ice forming in the hills   a moment
in which all is open   all connection
perspective   possibility

Pressing my palms
against the beaded glass
to touch   the amber patches
of other lives

Triptych

I

Nostalgia, blind drunkard   cannot enter
that London street   though I remember
windfalls fermented in the strip of garden
lilies of the valley in the palings' shade

We were oddities there
defined by what we did not have: television
deep-pile carpet, velvet-covered dining-room chairs
We lived in a mismatch among our books
in a house enfolded by a russet dusk
whose May buds slid into my parents' bedroom
and softly to them where they lay awake arguing
whispered   hush

It was a plain house   made plainer
now that the copper beech has been cut from its ground
succumbed to a sickness in the soil   or the neighbour
set against it in long campaign   won victory

for this was an ancient contest
and it was made for greatness
Its roots snaked back into archaic earth
Its destiny was greater than any house

II

In a garden split into two
we were half-barefoot children   wanderers
past bellflower and iris, overgrown lavender
the red hot pokers in the slumbering border

into a world of fruit canes, grubbed windfalls
into cutty grass and sticky yellow plums
grown wilder: danger underfoot   pears riven by wasps
blackberry loops run wild skirting the fence

and between the fences in the seeding grasses
in the gulch of the compost heap   in the strange
dark wood at the end of the garden
the wilderness grown miniature

III

The house
I recall now as a cave in which our lives rebounded
but there was light:
french doors opened into the summer garden
warmth fell in pools on our indoor books and games
or rain came, deliciously   caressing the panes
Doors slammed and were opened
or at the end of a summer day
we unlatched the window above the bath   called out
across the drive to our neighbours
so high up and such an odd place for a conversation
five laughing girls   five English voices

Language was a line strung between us, pegged
with sounds   gestures   games
the words we had grown used to
a tightrope we strolled across

Into the chaotic nest of the house
my father unleashed a tumult
which fissured the future I had been inventing
In the storm-wrecked hallway he dialled
and redialled   booking and cancelling departures

My own voice flailed against him
    I am English English English
    I won't go back

The family pod burst open and we parted

Dream Cities

I

Glasgow, late September   and the city I spoke of
in another country   (its fierce sandstone
burning, its bombast of finials built on the heads of slaves
the monumental tower blocks of a later order
catching fire from the west as a plane comes in)
has become in two months
a dream   a nostalgia

For it is litter   not grandeur
a muddied disturbance in a dirty river
a sullen reflection sliced by concrete
(the monumental pillars
and glorious boulevards of a later order)

Against the vivifying light
of the south   the suburban avenues
of a world of space   it is rain
rain   and old world pallor

and beyond it
on the high points of Aonach Mor and Ben Nevis
(so early   a door closing and opening)
the first snows of the winter

II

Early November   and the city I parted from
in two months has become a dream   technicolour
not quite Auckland or Christchurch
but a dream place of skyscrapers and heady blossom
stern waxy magnolia   silk of almond and crab apple
A dream place   but Christchurch as it was then

in mid-September   Jane driving me to the airport
past gardens reeking with nectar

for there Spring has continued without me

And here I wake   no longer at home

The World Egg

My mother has come to greet her daughters
Maggie from Middle Europe, I from rippled ocean
Briefly in the air-conditioned café
we share out sandwiches and cake as we used to
two between three   while
Maggie unloads her freight of gifts: a rose-cut box
from an antique shop in the Jewish quarter of Prague
a carved egg from Budapest

As my bag goes through the x-ray for the Glasgow flight
I'm called out   Something round
and dark, says the woman   Hollow

I don't say to her   It was a gift
I did not wrap it myself, Maggie
brought it for me from the heart of Europe
that ancient thoroughfare of tribes and rivalries
(for perhaps the heart is not a rose or a cup
but a street along which pass hidden centuries
of blood)

I simply unwrap its deeply carved
terracotta tree roots entwined in fierce earth

and it falls apart in my hands

(My heart does not break   it becomes
the cracked vessel containing all this)

It falls apart in my hands
into two hemispheres
lined with ceramic ocean   (Greenland's cobalt
and ice   the opalescent Pacific)

and at its centre   the airy and innocent tick
of beginnings

III

Petroglyphs

Petroglyphs
i.m. AGF

I

Hurled by voices spooled on a tape
out of the humdrum
into hectic glitter   headlights
brushing the brim of the road

there must have been snow
though I don't remember   a lightness
setting, like dried blood
from your brain's blocked artery

Black gave way to sodium glare
to where they said you could not know us
felt no pain   body afloat
mind closed to the erasing beam

but your breath
more anguished than a moth
rasped against the oxygen mask
a noisy spirit trapped in the lit glass

of a night we'd drive back into
luminous   freezing over
into the time of death

II

Winter   the road cut with straw
a pall of fires   sheep
carcasses, slaughtered cattle

Your body   gone up in smoke
sifted through our hands
ashes   we couldn't scatter

More than twenty years
you'd lived on a border
of limestone   millstone grit

Mewith Lane's lost dip
up onto the moor
Great Stone of Fourstones

or driving north
early morning over *Mallerstang*
to catch the light

solitary   with your camera
over *Winskill, Bowland Knotts*
In autumn when the crowds were gone

Dove Dale, Harter Fell
a catalogue of names
I never knew as you did

how the rivers made the land
watersheds
you felt under your footsoles

Later the roads I drove for you
crossing *the Buttertubs*
as if we crossed your palm

Four years after your death
handwritten on a post-it note
still stuck to the yellow

of the 1:25,000
I've walking to do, you tell me
at Airton-Kirkby Malham

III

Black and white
doorways   gateways
of dressed stone

parapets   rustications
a kerbstone's chiselled runnels
and off to the side of the city

a life of work   your own
and others   quarried dust
on the stonemason's apron

a spill of graphite from a desk
or in an old photograph
brick-dust in your grandfather's palm

turned to colour
pale as the shell mud
from which the barns were built

limestone dykes
still defining fields of green
light rippling over the fleece of sheep

pouring into the rectangle
of the photograph   a benediction
of water over rock

bubble of oxygen   wind/
blown grasses   frozen
ice   like light

Your camera
has become the past

We are tiny in the scope
of its steel plates:
sluice-gates through which light

breaks in a flood:
the whip of the flash exploding
the turbine of the film

your eye's stopped blink

IV

A room of books and stones
a window through which the moor enters
the weatherlight of your absence

V

Nickel ore from New Caledonia
Iron ore from Bourail district
bottled in glass *for the sour stomachs*
the heartburn of soldiers

Coral from the South Pacific
a circle of islands
Ironsand in hollow bamboo
stalactite from Waitomo

Talc from the Routeburn written in red chinagraph
a map of routes   the wave you walked on

Children born where they were making the dam
rock crystal from the clay pit at Coal Creek

Quartzite from Wanaka   pebbles
a handful of islands

Flint from Kentish fields   dark
as a breaking wave   an English spring

Hornstone from Lyme Bay   music the sailors love
to dance the waves we jumped to

Oolitic limestone   fish eggs *from the Cotswolds*
yellow cream as cakes
from *Archibald's in Oban*   peat in a paper bag

pebbled *sandstone from Stac Pollaidh*
Basalt from Trotternish   *quartz* flowering in it

pebble of *gabbro, Black Cuillin*
a piece of Skye   a blue ribbon   a childhood

Modified granite from Botallack mine
A black stone wrapped in paper   a woman's name
from years later   the end, almost, of a marriage
Granite from Lamorna   buried windows

Rock debris   pebbles
London clay from a tunnel heading below St Paul's

Iron ore from Swedish Lapland
Gneiss from Great Bernera
Schist from Easdale   flat, with nail heads

Millstone grit   Great Scar limestone
a yellow glue mark on granite   a lost label
All we can't know

Speckled *andesite from the English Lakes*
your first Christmas in England
a winter thrush among berries
but green   snow-scattered

Haematite from Ruddy Gill
Slate from Watendlath
Slate from Honister   a trace of ink
petrified flecks of label

from Rough Edge
below Kirkstone   your scattered ashes

VI

Your memorial
in the grassy graveyard
of the meeting house

your body turned to air and earth
a name on the wall
with the names of others

(those who belonged
through marriages
and families   generations)

Through the gate grass licks our feet
daffodils   lichen on gritstone
a date inscribed above us on a lintel

We glimpse benches   nothing
to speak of   silence
that might have given you peace

the clamour and jostled history
of the gravestones
come down to so few

a plain place   a view
you must once have loved
of the moor   a blue solitude

VII

Dear Dad,
your grand-daughter   eight years old
remembers your funny voices

My Mother's Body Interrogated by Light

This is what happened
Someone lifted a grey translucency to the light
and held it there
seeing the knit fracture in the clavicle
the branching ribs
the starry scatter of the bronchial tree
across the lung field   a cloudy shadow

The way when we were kids she'd call us down
to see a rain-swept spider's web
or against the kitchen window a leek sliced with light

This is what happened
Inside her body's driftwood coracle
she held her breath   her ribs coalesced
around a darkness they could read on a screen

The way she might have read the dark
of flint in chalk or a painting's thick colour

Meaning brought into light
a green circle
held by a membrane on a glass slide

.

This is what happened
The surgeon cut the echo of my mother's shoulder
conchoidal   bony with light

Her breath was a bird caught in the thoracic cage
The porous leaves that were the wings of birds
rustled as he parted the branches
the ropes of the sail that shadowed the lung

In the cavity of her body
his hands with their instruments
tethered the branches   drew knotted filaments
around the artery   the venous trunks
the cartilaginous rings of the bronchial tree

The way her fingers threading a skein of colour
anchored patterns, jottings, silks
the names of children   a network of reminders
the memorial lattice of the living

His wrists in the ribs' net   he cut death out
lifted it in its darkened flap clear of the body

The hands with their curved steel catching bone
threading filaments through muscle
resealing the fatty layers   the unpeeled skin
might have been the hands of a crew mending a sail
that would float her out beyond the nodule
that new thing as strange as any flint picked up a beach

The way she'd waited once for a cocoon to hatch
a butterfly to struggle out   breath
rippling the skeins   the netted wing
of the scapula lifting   a lacy shadow

.

This is what happened
before we knew that her hands would stiffen as twigs
that her brain would fail to solve the intricacies of a knot

before we knew that the nodule had seeded itself
invisibly along the branches of the blood
moving in that colour we see now when we lift our hands
instrumentless   to the light

A Flowering
i.m. GFF

Hunting
in a clutter of trowels and bean canes
for a cyclamen laid on its side
on the shelf is a space   nothing
though I see it   in the chaos
of my mind's eye   come sidelong to it
out of the corner of the eye   the lost
flame of it   the lost white fire

a flowering
in the green dusk of that room
or was it underwater
that place where death was
your death   your particular death?

All winter a sculpture of fizzing optics
shimmered at the edge of dust light
the outward push of it
beauty singing in the brain
the heart-shaped cluster   green and silver
the purple underside   the slender stalks
the upward push of the fleshy crown
out of its shining plastic

All winter it flowered
pushing outward against the brain stem
the glowing filaments of the cranial nerves

the swept-up movement of the petals
into the cool green room
of a house you no longer lived in

All winter an imperceptible pressure
against the nerves that corded your spine
netting lungs   fingertips
the bulbed veined leaf of your heart
filaments of thought enclosed
movement   heartbeat   breath slowed

The way the flower lifts and doesn't fall
like your hand in the bed
in the weeks of your dying   caught upwards
in mid-air   stilled

A Poem of Blood and the Body

for Sallie

To call you back from death
as if we called you in from the rain
a girl caught in briars
not the barbed wire forest of thorns
the headache that made you scream

To call you back
more than twenty years
to the steamy sauna: naked
and at ease   talking
blood rites then   our feminism
bound up with our bodies
our daughters' first menstruations
still in the future
—we'll celebrate, you said

not the traumatic traffic of your arteries
the space under your skull that filled
with blood   split your head with lights
bright as briars that struck you blind

but your bright voice, Sallie
your quick, funny, American mind

To call you back
through all the years the moon shone on
to your kitchen's bright newness
the steam of Jon's cooking   the plume
of smoke from your cigarettes
making it as fumy as that dreamy room
we used to fill with meandering talk

broken   by this

the epicentre of an earthquake   shiver
of pain that skewered you
until you screamed
and the ambulance   delivering you
through the swish of doors
to where you sank, came back
through aftershocks that shook your body
unpapered its cracks
—you were a lute unstrung

In the torn hours of the morning
in which your body lay   soundless
instrument lit by an artificial spark
those who loved you
put their hands in darkness
to forms and mourning
inked the blood stilled in the tubes
delivered you to the surgeon's art

The doors were closed
the surgeon's hands cut
as if from a house opened to night
your body's parts   tokens gentled
to kidney dishes, ice boxes
precious treasure to other living bodies

Why should I call it loss
others alive with the best wish
of your beloveds?   Gifts
transported like funeral flowers
in all their elements except

the body that was their one element
that bound you, Sallie
in your quick bright life

Birds Enter It

Closed to us, not by railings
black iron bars of rain
falling into mud   unwitnessed

imagine her   half-turned
clicking the remote on her car
the beam locked invisibly into the rain

the rough bulk of his body
only a man asking directions
on a twilit pavement

faceless   but only a man
who stopped her, dragged her
a thread caught on black iron bars

rain falling as she fought him
her life's insignia scattered into grass
the closed space of the earth

Petals, leaves, winged seeds
her coverlet where
white-overalled officers kneel

questioning the crushed grass
the shadows of the park
the black iron of sunlight

fallen   across our own green hearts

On a Day of Sunshine

After you'd departed
bearing the darkness you cannot let go of
    the weight of a drowned boy
    pulled from water on a day of sunshine

in the garden where yesterday's gale
had blown its trumpet unheralded
    (from half-opened windows seemed
    only a bluster   a green whirligig)

I found under scattered hawthorn
    the full tilt of its playful somersaults
    the beanstalks' angular striations
    bent, broken   still lucent if held to light

In sunshine I knelt to tie the tender green
    too late   the frilled, unfurling leaves
    the velvet and inky petals

their lobes stabbed purple   seeped
filling unstoppably with dark water

IV

Lucky Heart

Heart Sounds

Soundings   depths   sonar
Is this what she heard
tuning her ear to your heart
    as if to a shell
swirling in its breathy closure
    the sea's whisper

who long ago
    when you were a foundling
rocked in a basket of kelp
listened through my blood's tides
    to your minuter heart
pulsing its percussive undersong

Is this what she heard
    echo its turbulent vibrato
in a tumult of playful voices
Through the valves of your hot heart
salt blood boomed
    in its cave of murmurs

    a rumour
that the heart is a drum   difficult
remorselessly navigating
its own   divergent rhythms

A Small Failure of Love

Ten days before Christmas we're not writing cards
(you rakishly forming your letters
pencil arcing to havoc and play)

I'm helping you to glue up a castle
cutting up cartons   but mostly drowning
in the flotsam of fridge shelves

yoghurts, broccoli, mustard, junk food
jars half-emptied of the supermarketed world's
sun-dried jetsam

The sink's a glacier   (We had fun with this
steam I warned you of cooled in the ice cave
to a fume of dragon's breath)

The floor's a ship-wrecked deck
of damp cloths, soda grit   lit from a plastic box
lined with butter papers, tumbled garlic bulbs

Way past lunchtime   you're hungry
The ice dragon sings in her cave
You keep telling me   I keep answering

Won't be long, not space for a breadboard even
so when you slip   go flying
on dappled underwater linoleum

I don't even think   Sweetheart
I yell   What now?   and you say
Don't be angry with me Mummy   my knee's hurting

It takes me so long to let go
of the ship-wrecked jars and bottles   It takes so long
and something lost   while you waited for me

In the Map of the Palm
for Freya

The city   my life in it
comparative   an arc
of photographs taken at 70 mph
at 60, 50   slowing
blurred light stilled to colour
flaunts a bravado of distance
as we come in towards the bridge
that'll vault us
over a river that's less
than its noisy history   the clash

and beat of hammered rivets
in which I'm a stranger
the years I've lived here
weightless   without scale
on the map of the palm
hardly a clink in a voicebox
Glasgow   just a spinning galaxy
where I've come to land
anglophone   a recognisable alien

But you   my lightfoot dancer
my Scottish daughter
are at home
in your own childhood
Your toys and paints and shells
spill from red sandstone
dug from Ayrshire   yellow fennel
against a weatherboard garage
a blue scooter passed to you
on the tireless chain of children

and far-flung from a shelf of braes
the city I catch sight of

through the windscreen
glaikit, shifting through the net
of the wire horse you farewell
as I   circumscribed by mirrors
pull into the lane
that'll take us across the border

The horse is a sentinel
You greet it   coming home
at the end of a summer
of crossing borders and water

to a house
from which the spokes of your life
flick outward to futures
spun from light   like videotape
but memory
a child   and a city
in the net of your palm

Lucky Heart

for Fran

It might have been
a Christmas tree bauble
spun glass patterned with gold
a bubble blown by a child
floating its airy spectrum
into jostled sunlight

It might have been
colour dredged from palettes
graphite and a black sheep's
twisted wool   deep-dyed
scraps of your weaving
but it was blood   not art

the clotted thickness
that swirled your life's detritus
did not lose its mass   turn to air
a popped bubble of light
it passed through the hoop
of your lucky heart

Sudden Darting Crested

Into the morning quiet
waxwings   vivid-crested   clash
until glass reverberates

with the chirr of the thrush in the rowan
crazy for berries   holds his own
eye on the crested mob

The waxwings roost   they swoop
and wheel in the language of flight
They inhabit a space

beyond the windswept garden
the step where my neighbour meditates

the door at which his wife appears
gold and magenta, an exotic species

What has irrupted into their lives?
She crosses the damp winter lawn
arms full of words   their bodies

urgent in the rainy garden
messengers across an earthbound space

in which I too try to construct
a language of happiness

oblique   small   sidelong
it also makes
these sudden, darting, crested shapes

of arms   that might be
weighted with flowers

Dream Catcher

Light enters   but barely
pulses over the rough skins of pears
their russet bulging into fog
echoes the mistle thrushes' speckle
in the cold beyond the window

Impossible to believe
that elsewhere   the sky
might be a grabbed blue handful
of winter light   miraculous
as a magician's silk handkerchief

Impossible to believe
the world is not rapt in this quiet
the clock hand annotates
in its plain speech
the hard disk's humdrum

Catching my late lunch
beside a sill of sheafed paintings
a sea serpent
feathered dream catcher
bird of your making

in these minutes of quiet
before I wrap myself
in the thick materials of winter
to bring you home
through folded cloud

on my mind, child
your small body at our bedside
throat hurting   taken in to sleep
while I drifted   awake in a blue
beyond this fog of privacy

In the playground
you load me with your school bag
broken-strapped
You've shaken off your cold—
ready to run in your shirt sleeves
have gone off   pell mell

to inhabit a few more hours
of playfulness and racket
snatched
            from this quiet
that I reoccupy in late afternoon

                unbroken
by your bright bird chatter

(like the fisherman's wife
granted a wish)

            this odd quiet
in which no one reinvents me

V

The Language of Memory

Pilot

In another season
he could pinpoint the summits
the passes between them   skipped
gullies   the cliffs' vertiginous riffs
        a mapped scribble of rock
        over which he plies his art

        He knows the chart
but now he flies a terrain
obliterated by snowfall
the mountains God's mistake
lochans null grey   ridges erased
corries turned to violet shadow
rims fanning out from icefall
over which windslab plates   fractures
to a blank   in which he's alone

            and all he knows
is the air rush he moves in
even the wind gives no quarter
the sky a perfect blue
clueless as the white beneath him
not even a comb of cirrus
tarnishes its thinning mirror
        Astray in finned aluminium
        he has forgotten   who he is

            or what he knows
kept alive by numbers, readings
the lights of the instrument panel

the forest   lifting its living needles
        to rescue him

Animal

Our tracks sink where the sun's
metallic sheen unsettles the snow
to prints lighter than our own

not yet melted to cupped blue
petalled paw prints
too round for a mountain hare

a dog astray from human habitation
or a fox straight-lining
up beyond the urban margin

What we see is a pattern
a joy of exploration like our own
Sunstruck

we don't imagine
hunger   a jumped crack of the jaws
blood on a licked muzzle

Our own imagination
tricks us with a soundless beast
its tracks   no certain sign

of any traveller over frozen quagmire
Is this cognisance
the alchemy of snow?

It runs without us   crosses easily
into our habitat of fuss and frosted grass
enters by the rent between worlds

has already entered
perceived us   by clumsy tracks
we have not yet made

Winter Garden

What confounds me in the garden
    what disables me   past
the heartless late-winter sprigs   sharp
cold earth   rim of sleet frozen
to the trampoline's metallic hulk

    is a failure of form
to find from dry sticks and shuttered buds
from undug, grass-choked borders   edgeless lawn
    a shape

as of
trees in the distant park   in layered mist
perfectly structured

What overwhelms me is the living thing
grown in time   wayward   makes
bushes trees   greedy for light   In their shade
the lost   grown sideways
        ugly, leafless, knotted
        is this the garden I made?

There is no beauty in it   the buds
are not beauty   the delicate stars of moss
are not   nor the slender spears
these are no more than misapprehensions

It is all failure   the misshapen magnolia
pruned too late for form
an ugly cat's cradle over

the purple and pale heads of the Lenten roses
The only brazen thing   they do not
console me

The Language of Memory (The Bees)

Are they memory
    the bees on her hand
    held in amber on the sunlit
camber of the beach
    as if they'd swarmed

scattering their gold black fur?
She has no fear of them
nor they of her   fair strands
of flying hair   her hand
with its warmth of sand

Were they cupped
in a globe of trickling grains
    or did she lift each one
    by the shimmering
folded lens of its wings?

Are they memory   or its gaps?
The day's ornate surface
a cracked glaze   the bees
on her hand   gold and black
fragments of their own erasure

Fibre-optic

A man   a woman   a child
in a sunlit interior
The man's eyes stream
with cold   his nose is red
he closes his eyes in the sunlight
The child plays with her toys   sings
to herself and to them   makes
voices   in a circle of sunlight
The woman without a book   becalmed
thinks she hears music   sees
the inner and outer fabrics
of this place   steel structure
glass skin beyond which
in sunlit winter sharpness
visitors to a concrete garden
are people in movement   They
live in time   in the music she thinks
she hears   a beat
a resonance   a plant unfolding
its music   growth laps   over
laps   suspended by the invisible
strings of connection
art made of time   composed
it unfolds to the woman
a language without translation

A Proprioceptive Manifesto

Learning to re-read
the unconscious information
of joint and tendon
to hold my position in space
briefly balanced
above my torn calf muscle
the splayed bones of the ankle

am I teaching my body to know its place?

In London when I was nine
my voice mumming its new vowels
other-footed   antipodean still
I pulled my socks off on the way to school

Forty years on
here is my bare New Zealand foot
here are my flexible bones

what I am   in the body

my position in space
in Scotland
the week before my fiftieth birthday

What I didn't tell you
was what happened
before the overstretch
on the blue-swept heathery slope
what happened
before I mistook my step
put my foot wrong   (land
slips   the torn
hillside's gouts of flying grass)

thinking over and over   the nature
of poetry   the bare speech
of the body

What is this thing we do in words?

the breath   balanced
the feet walking

          the body of the poem

the balance organ of the inner ear

in no other way
but this

the declaration of ourselves

Lightning Source UK Ltd.
Milton Keynes UK
UKOW03f1928070414

229551UK00001B/35/P